THE FULFILLED PROMISE

JEREMY WRIGHT

Hidden Meadows: The Fulfilled Promise

©2022 Jeremy Wright

Print ISBN: 978-1-66785-469-4

eBook ISBN: 978-1-66785-470-0

Dedicated to:

Vickie M. Wright

Jeremy B. Wright

Future Generations

Anyone Who Desires a Life of Peace and Purpose

Book Intention and Harvest of 1,000 Generations

The intention of this book is to recognize what is at stake in life when we do not have peace and purpose. In addition, this book aims to emphasize the importance of trusting the process, releasing to receive, and chasing purpose. These themes are essential, because they help keep us grounded on the journey of peace and purpose. Through time and chance, opportunities present themselves and, depending on where we are in our journey, our decisions create alternate routes, although still with the destination of peace and purpose. Everything in life becomes more vivid when you realize that living the life you deserve and what future generations will inherit is on the other side of inner peace and honoring your purpose in life.

When we do not trust the process, survival instincts kick in, forcing us to make decisions that are not from a place of peace or in alignment with our purpose in life: we are simply trying to survive. When we do not release to receive, we allow what has been keeping us from inner peace to occupy the space necessary for circumstances and people to help mold and shape us for our purpose in life. When we do not have a consistent experience with inner peace or chasing our life's purpose, our life has meaning based on the decisions of our outcome: survival. A life of peace and purpose allows seeds to be planted that will create an endless harvest, allowing us to live the life we deserve and ensure a solid foundation for future generations. We must remember to plant seeds with good intentions and without concern about how and when they bloom.

Peace creates separation from things that are fleeting during and after this human experience. Purpose gives meaning to life, depth to our experiences, and helps the world become better than when we got here. Given that life and sometimes our decisions limit our time to reflect, I felt it best that we revisit what we have talked about in previous books within this series to see what's at stake beyond our individual lives. The conscious and consistent choice to live a life of peace and purpose can create the life we deserve and an abundant harvest for 1,000 generations.

Dear Me,

Let's go back to the unseen places. Dare to turn over every rock, lift up every carpet, and re-examine every shattered piece. We must do this knowing the impact it can have on our present life and future generations. Choosing a life of peace and purpose has had challenging moments, but has proven worth every step. From a place of peace, honoring our purpose in life allows us to create the life we deserve.

It's not about how and when it will happen, but knowing that abundance is our portion with the positive intent we have sown in every seed we have planted. A life of abundance can be quickly taken away, and it's up to us to ensure we have done our part to be ready to handle it. Maximizing this human experience is an opportunity many may feel is too heavy a lift, but we can lighten the load. Let's continue our journey of peace and purpose, knowing that abundance is on the other side. Not for materialistic gain, but for the fulfillment of our purpose, leaving the world a better place for the generations to come.

With all the unconditional love from within,
The ME behind me

Dear Reader,

I am still on my journey of peace and purpose, and I am making progress. A part of what keeps me motivated is knowing the impact the decisions in my life will have on future generations. In writing this book, I hope you also realize what is at stake when we do not live a life of peace and purpose. It's fair to live your life how you decide to live it; it is your life. I encourage you to look deeply inside yourself to examine the underlying reason for any decisions you make during this human experience, and ask yourself: *Why am I making the choices I am making?*

Even the most minor decision, one we think is nothing, can suggest a tie to behaviors from conditioning, trauma, or even prior generations. This small glimmer of awareness is just enough to encourage our behaviors, although focused on self, to have positive intent given the indirect influence they may have on others. At a minimum, choose to live a life of peace so that those around you can do the same. If you should be so daring, adding purpose can positively shift your life in ways unimaginable. Abundance is within each opportunity, if we dare to embark on the journey of peace and purpose.

With all of the unconditional love that I have,

Jeremy

Author Updates

Keeping the intent of this book in mind, why have I not gotten to the place where I am allegedly supposed to be? It's approximately 11:11 p.m. on May 20, 2022, and I am in the hospital waiting room. By now, I am supposed to be happily married and doing all of the necessary work for a lifelong commitment, living in a different country, debt-free, traveling the world whenever my husband and I desire for however long we want to; in the process of retiring my mom from work, and at this present moment I am supposed to be in Tucson, Arizona, for graduation, but life happens. As I sort through a myriad of emotions, one thing keeps happening: I block my ability to experience the full spectrum of emotions from the circumstances I find myself in. As I have said in all of my books, I am human. I still have a lot of work and inner healing. Yes, the person writing a series about peace and purpose is still healing.

In reflecting from a place of peace, my ability to empathize with others often gets in the way of expressing my emotions. No doubt, this is still tied to conditioning, trauma, consistently broken promises, and so much more. These past circumstances that involved people resulted from decisions made in a place without inner peace or alignment with life's purpose. With a lifespan of thirty-two years, I am still dealing with the impacts of things that happened ten to twenty years ago. Imagine what the generation before me went through without awareness or access to resources such as mental health professionals.

This visual of the crippling effect from generation to generation helps focus on what is at stake when we do not go on our individual journeys of peace and purpose. Through self-awareness and leveraging these three themes—discussed in previous books of the Peace and Purpose series—we can stay grounded and consistently make choices to get our desired outcomes. What happens when I sort out my life and that of the generation before me so that, at a minimum, I have peace? The next generation—consisting of my children, godchildren, family, and community—reaps the benefits of lessons learned from others. On paper, this seems so easy, but you can see how difficult this is.

Now that I am not juggling so many things, I am doing something that I rarely do: reading other bodies of work while writing my own, specifically Viola Davis's *Finding Me* and Brené Brown's *Atlas of the Heart: Mapping Meaningful Connection and the Language of Human Experience*. It's crazy how things fall into your lap at just the right time. What I love about Viola Davis's book is that I immediately identified that we both have roots in South Carolina, we both lived a life of trauma and shame due to the life experiences of generations before us, and we both are doing the work to get back to our truest selves. I admire her authentic and transparent body of work because it helps people like me realize anything is possible. As I read Brené Brown's book, I am learning the importance of being clear about what you are experiencing emotionally to navigate the path forward.

Knowing and processing what is at stake, I commit to really getting to the root of my triggers and allowing myself to be human and allow myself to experience the full spectrum of emotions; I am not the machine trauma, and survival has conditioned me to be. I am proud of myself for having defined my peace and identifying my purpose in life, but consistency in my behaviors is where I can improve. Again, almost three decades of my own stuff plus the weight of the stuff from generations before me creates a heavy load for my life. Reshaping my physical lens or my perspective on everyday life takes work. Still, it is a necessary step to ensure that the generations after me reap the harvest that will sustain them long after I am gone. My individual life is the stepping-stone to countless lives beyond mine. While giving myself grace, I bear this burden to be consistent with inner peace and purpose with pride so that those behind me can live abundantly.

Abundance

To me, abundance is not always tangible. I feel that abundance can take many forms, yet what is consistent is opportunity. Two days ago, May 16, 2022, was a lunar eclipse; however, I didn't get the opportunity to see it due to a stormy night. Among a group chat inspired by divine chaos, I was able to see the moon from someone else's perspective. Although I didn't have the opportunity to see the moon that night, others did.

I did have the opportunity to witness a cleansing rain mixed with thunder and lightning. It was a moment of healing and clearing the way. The opportunity that I was hoping to have turned into something else. Someone else's clear night is another's opportunity to sift through cloudiness, leading to a necessary cleansing. Tonight, as I was walking at midnight, I noticed the moon. I witnessed a few sleeping ducks, a small heron, and what could have been a dinosaur, a huge crane.

As I kept walking, the moon peeked through the clouds and the buildings as if it was playing hide and seek. From my perspective, the moon didn't change; I did. It provided a profound epiphany: When we think opportunities should present themselves, they do, but not always in a way that makes sense or is evident, like a clear night. Regardless of how it shows up, it is still an opportunity to attain abundance through our decisions that hopefully align with a life of peace and purpose. Regardless of what happens in life, our perspective and actions produce an outcome; it's truly up to us to trust the process, release to receive, and chase purpose.

In this next season of my life, I will make conscious and consistent choices to jump headfirst into opportunities on this journey of peace and purpose. From a place of peace, not worrying about the how and when, I will do the best I can with what I have at any given time. I know that time and chance will continuously cross, creating opportunities for me to align the essence of who I am—spiritually and as a human being—with my purpose. My desire to honor my purpose will leverage divine chaos through time and chance, bringing circumstances and people that help ready me for and propel me toward opportunities. On the other side of my conscious and consistent choice to jump into opportunity, guided by peace and purpose, is abundance in all its forms.

The Journey of
Peace and Purpose

In previous books within this series, rest constructs I label as "books" of life, self, love, and meditation. These constructs are then broken into components labeled as "chapters" with quotes and affirmations/mantras to help make them more understandable. My hindsight summary and, of course, reflection and application are provided to ensure you apply what we talk about, allowing you to connect the dots at your own pace. I reorganized these constructs and components like puzzle pieces to create a comprehensible picture to make a life of peace and purpose easy for anyone to attain. Before we break things down, and now that I am at the end of this phase of the Peace and Purpose series, let me share a high-level overview of my journey of peace and purpose.

After picking up the pieces from my response to a series of traumatic events, I realized life was much bigger than survival. I began to embrace that I had a unique reason to be alive. My highest sense of self stepped forward to guide me towards inner peace and purpose without me knowing it. As I put together the pieces and discarded what was no longer needed, I recognized a connection between the lessons I learned from circumstances and people and my gifts and talents; my purpose. I could only do this based on my new perspective that was formed through operating from a place of inner peace and seeing circumstances and people as a means of preparing me for my purpose.

Now realizing life was a process, I set out on a journey of self where I was forced to accept the core of who I was and accept people at their core, knowing that our interactions were readying one another for our individual purpose or what we asked for knowingly and unknowingly. Sometimes these interactions with people kept me in a cycle of survival or drained me of my capacity to go further down my journey of self, requiring me to eventually establish boundaries. As a part of establishing boundaries to ensure I had enough capacity to pour my purpose, I had to define things like love to measure peoples' actions better, including my own actions.

Creating boundaries rooted in what I defined things as created space and a sense of accountability to do the internal work necessary to be able to handle my purpose. My journey of self made it easier for me to communicate and understand the importance of needs allowing me to interact with people differently, especially knowing they carried lessons with them. Once I set all my thoughts, words, and deeds towards honoring my purpose, with more space and capacity, life had a flow about it. I could now begin pouring my purpose in different ways.

Inner peace undoubtedly taught me that I was connected to or a part of something that created the human experience. I figured I could leverage that power with positive intent to make honoring my purpose easier through manifestation. If I was operating from a place of peace, I knew I could design my life through my decisions that were always about purpose. My goal was to ground myself in the present moment to allow my highest sense of self to step forward, allowing me to be with the creator of this human experience. This allowed me to see, hear, think, and understand clearly so that I knew what was required of me and which decisions to make as I lived. When I spent time in my place of inner peace, I allowed my creativity to see precisely what I wanted in alignment with my purpose. I allowed the feeling invoked during visualization, in addition to maintaining the right posture, to be a part of my decision-making as I lived.

Now, five years into this journey of peace and purpose, I have honored my purpose by being an author, coach, and speaker; everything is in order. I choose purpose at work, home, during times of conflict, and during moments of rest by operating from a place of peace. I didn't try to control how or when things happened, I allowed my highest sense of self to step forward to make the best decisions, knowing that I would manifest my purpose and thus the life I deserved. The difference between hard work and manifesting are the ingredients used. Hard work is an external experience while manifesting is an internal experience that demonstrates alignment and flow. In addition to blood, sweat, and tears used for hard work are the additional ingredients for manifesting, leveraging the entire human and spiritual experience with the power of what created the experience.

Purpose is my magnet that I use to attract circumstances and people. I continue to operate from a place of inner peace lowering any personal ask, energy, or vibrations that life would use as direction to contradict manifesting my purpose. While in alignment with the creator of life or source, I do my best to allow my highest sense of self to make decisions during this human experience. This helps my thoughts, words, and deeds to be in alignment with purpose creating flow. Now that I have shared my experience with you; let's get to work.

Book of Life

Life is so quick. We were trying to say our first words one minute, then walking across the stage for graduation, jobs, marriage, children, divorce, death, and more. These life experiences—some perceived as good, bad, and ugly—are continuously reorienting us back toward finding peace within ourselves and honoring a larger purpose to be of service to people. Because we are trying to survive, looking through a physical or survival lens, we cannot perceive the circumstances and people as the lessons and preparation they are. Having an idea of how life works helps lay a foundation for the journey of peace and purpose; this in turn yields an abundant life through consistency and positive intentions.

- *Chapter of the Bigger Picture*

  - Quote   "We are more connected than we admit; harming you is like harming myself, disrupting life and its process." (*Love and Meditation: The Keys to Manifestation*, p. 56)

  - Mantra—I live my life knowing that I will receive the outcomes of my own behavior.

- *Chapter of Purpose*

  - Quote—"My soul bears my purpose as a gift to the world I was born in." (*Well to the Soul: Pouring from a Full Vessel*, p. 16)

- o Mantra—Every day, I wake up to honor my purpose; to be of service to others is fulfilling.

- *Chapter of Life as a Process*

  - o Quote—"No matter how or when you bring water to a boil, one must have and use everything necessary to make it happen; trust the process." (*Lenses: Seeing the Unseen Spaces Between Us,* p. 15)

  - o Mantra—I trust the process and allow it to unfold without concern about the how and when.

- *Chapter of Forming My Lens*

  - o Quote—"I can see a lot and still not understand until its meaning is revealed." (*Lenses: Seeing the Unseen Spaces Between Us,* p. 24)

  - o Mantra—I am forever evolving to become my best self; my perspective and understanding evolve with me.

Hindsight

Knowing that peace and purpose are at stake, I understand why life is the way it is. Peace and purpose cannot be given to you; they must be earned through self-awareness, commitment to self, reflection, accountability, and grit (SCRAG). It is the individual's choice to go through life as they please, but I encourage everyone to step out of survival mode and go on the journey of peace and purpose. I feel that what keeps people in survival mode is the lack of self-awareness, and that is not necessarily their own fault. The more self-aware a person is, the more they have space between themself and what happens during this human experience to see they are a part of something bigger.

Without self-awareness, there would be no opportunity to see the deeper meaning of things to attain peace or to see how one's purpose sits at the intersection of lessons learned, gifts, talents, and being of service to people. Being able to sift through what we perceive as chaos allows us to develop the proper perspective, have the strength and stamina necessary to endure life experiences, and apply learned lessons to our decisions to attain peace and purpose. Without awareness, we would just see circumstances as life and stay in cycles passed from generation to generation, unfortunately allowing peace and purpose to escape us. This is why it is essential to trust the process and allow things to unfold without trying to control the how and when.

Our lives have conditioned us to keep thinking about what's next when we should really focus on what's now. This is due to the ongoing battle of systems versus humanity versus nature. Until someone has SCRAG to break free, they will always live in the past or future, allowing peace and purpose to escape them. Lock yourself into the present moment to see that the journey of peace and purpose is happening right before your eyes. Recognize that you play a significant role in the bigger picture of the human experience by honoring your purpose. Through self-awareness, trust that things are happening the way they should while making the best decision you can from a place of clarity.

Allowing yourself to evolve into a new way of thinking or seeing things from the right lens is necessary, as how you were conditioned, raised, or taught may not fit now. What better way to have someone honor their purpose than to find peace within themselves while enduring the chaos we encounter to mold and shape us during this human experience. This approach allows peace and purpose to become embedded in who we are, preventing things from derailing us compared to having a foundation built on things that are based on survival. Tangible abundance takes tremendous sacrifice. Allowing time and chance to create opportunities in which individuals make favorable decisions can create the life they deserve, if and only if they find inner peace and purpose.

Reflection

To ensure you understand the book of life and recognize what is at stake if you do not pursue inner peace and the purpose of your life, reflect on the following:

1. How do I play a part in the reason I believe people exist?

2. After finding the connection between the ingredients of purpose (my learned life lessons, gifts, and talents), how can I be of service to people?

3. What can I start, stop, and keep doing, knowing that life is a process that I must trust?

4. How might my perspective and understanding need to evolve, given that I accept that life is a process and that circumstances and people condition me to be ready for my purpose?

Application

After reflecting on your answers to the above questions, journal about these responses for at least fifteen minutes per day. If you need more time to reflect and journal, do so; this is your opportunity to check your understanding of life and what's at stake when a journey of peace and purpose is not taken.

Book of Self

We are born into this world as individuals, and must focus on ourselves so that we are secure in who we are as we experience life. Knowing that being secure in who you are is a foundation to peace and the ability to honor purpose, commitment to going too deep and dark places that we stray away from is crucial for healing. Our purpose is only successful when we are deeply rooted in and at peace with our true selves. Choosing not to show up as your best self means risking being able to live the life you deserve and the lives of those that follow. A journey of self can prove to be the most difficult, but is a fulfilling part of the journey to peace and purpose.

- *Chapter of Acceptance*

  - Quote—"I did not have a choice to be born. I do have a choice in how I show up every day. I choose to be secure in who I am; there is no other way." (*Well to the Soul: Pouring from a Full Vessel,* p. 30)

  - Mantra—I am in love with the core of who I am and how I show up every day.

- *Chapter of The Human Spectrum*

  - Quote—"Our uniqueness and imperfection qualify us as human; anyone who challenges another opens their soul like a window." (*Well to the Soul: Pouring from a Full Vessel,* p. 26)

- ○ Mantra—How I see other people reflects where I am in my personal journey.

- *Chapter of Boundaries*

  - ○ Quote—"A boundary is a request for protection from one person to another." (*Well to the Soul: Pouring from a Full Vessel,* p. 34)

  - ○ Mantra—I have healthy boundaries to maintain my peace and capacity to chase purpose.

- *Chapter of Pouring*

  - ○ Quote—"What I am pouring into will carry the intention and condition in which I pour. I pour when my intention and condition are right so that what I pour into can grow." (*A Gift of Peace and Purpose: A Survivor's Journey,* p. 42)

  - ○ Mantra—I am pouring my purpose as a gift to the world, watering seeds that will bloom.

Hindsight

Knowing that peace and purpose are at stake, I understand why a journey of self is needed. How can one find inner peace and honor their purpose when they do not accept themselves as they are? Imagine if the bee didn't accept how it was designed; what would happen to life as we know it? Imagine if the tree didn't accept the seasons; what would happen to life as we know it? Inner peace settles us into who we are meant to be at our core to honor our purpose. This is why acceptance of self is essential.

Everything that was required for you to be you—including the decision of your families, schooling, life decisions, and more—have created you to be a unique individual. Your uniqueness is what qualifies only you to honor your purpose, as no one else can do the same. Acceptance of self doesn't mean that you stay where you are but that you are in love with the core of who you are. The intangible aspects of who you are must reside in a place of peace to reflect on the outside and, more importantly, in your behaviors. This same level of acceptance of self should include accepting people for who they are.

Again, this doesn't mean that we should stay as we are, not growing and evolving to become the best version of ourselves but see and accept people for where they are. Give people what you would want to be given. After all, we need each other on our individual journeys of peace and purpose as we bring about lessons intended to prepare us for peace and purpose. There are more than seven billion people on this planet we call earth, and the thought that anything other than cohesion is the solution to our problems is acceptance of the inevitable, a dying of the human experience. It takes inner peace for people to grasp and act on helping one another in life.

Even though we need to help one another get through life, healthy boundaries ensure that we can meet our individual needs and then the needs of others. How can you give what you do not have to give? Boundaries are a way of asking the next person to give you space and grace so that you can honor your needs. Anything else is giving yourself permission to attain peace and purpose with the leftover capacity of what other people take from you; this will get you nowhere really fast.

Understanding life and the journey of self helps with peace and purpose because it shows how you must be present and play an active role in your own life. Without this balance of living life and digging deeper to understand the meaning of circumstances, peace cannot be attained and purpose cannot be identified or used while being of service to others. Abundance cannot occur where there is no opportunity for it to be planted as a seed and nurtured; your purpose in action makes this possible. Remember, the ingredients to the recipe that make your purpose are lessons learned, gifts, and talents. On the journey of peace and purpose, you must spend time with yourself to understand yourself and embrace who you are, as your uniqueness qualifies you to be the piece you are in the bigger picture of the human experience; others must do the same in their own lives. With a solid foundation and security in who you are, reflections about interactions between those we share this human experience with, healthy boundaries, inner peace, and purpose can create a life of abundance.

Reflection

To ensure you understand the book of self and recognize what is at stake if you do not pursue inner peace and the purpose of your life, reflect on the following:

1. Given that I must heal myself and evolve in some areas, what must I accept about my life and myself, knowing that my uniqueness qualifies me to honor my purpose?

2. Knowing that the collective human experience is God or source, and the only way I can be prepared for my purpose is through circumstances that bring lessons, what must I start, stop, and keep doing when interacting with people?

3. What boundaries must I set to restore, strengthen, increase, and protect my capacity to honor my purpose and live life as I please?

4. What is my indication that I am in a balanced place to pour my purpose, being of service to people and making the world better?

Application

After reflecting on your answers to the above questions, journal about these responses for at least fifteen minutes per day. If you need more time to reflect and journal, do so; this is your opportunity to check your understanding of self and what's at stake when a journey of peace and purpose is not taken.

Book of Love

During this human experience, we must interact with others and, in some cases, ourselves. Knowing how to properly navigate these interactions makes life easier. This is best done from a place of inner peace and knowing how purpose becomes attainable through the molding and shaping that life provides through circumstances and people. Although these interactions are not always what we desire, they are necessary, as we are more connected than we realize. Knowing how to navigate life when dealing with people allows future generations to be prepared for the actual world, not discussed in the systems they will become integrated into.

- *Chapter of Love*

  - Quote—"I love myself enough to show you that how I define love is essential to our relationship." (*Love and Meditation: The Keys to Manifestation*, p.18)

  - Mantra—I allow myself to experience the full spectrum of love.

- *Chapter of Communication*

  - Quote—"I chose to shape the sound from my lips to wrap around the shape of your heart." (*Love and Meditation: The Keys to Manifestation*, p.12)

  - Mantra—I am communicating for understanding and not to be heard.

- *Chapter of Needs*

  - Quote—"People's needs are the framework for operating at their best self." (*Love and Meditation: The Keys to Manifestation*, p.17)

  - Mantra—I am fulfilling my core needs to be my best self.

Hindsight

Knowing that peace and purpose are at stake, I understand why love is needed during this human experience. Interactions are not always easy, whether with family, friends, or strangers. It becomes more challenging to manage when there is an investment of precious resources. Love is what you define it as, but it must start with self. Laying a foundation of love with things that are external to you makes it possible for whatever is built on the foundation to be easily broken.

The journey of self is also attributed to love, as on this journey you fall in love with the essence of who you are at your core. When you have defined and created a solid foundation of love, rooted in self, how you process love when dealing with family and friends shifts. I have to keep reminding myself to watch people's words and, more importantly, actions. Actions are what help give context to words beyond what your norms or lens have allowed you to interpret. This makes it easier to communicate when there is a disconnection between parties, including yourself.

Knowing the full context and how people operate ensures a better probability of getting the intent of your message across. Consider what may be endured on a journey of self for all parties involved. Use that as a visual of what your message must get through for the intent of your message to be received. In addition to what you visualize as layers of what your message must break through, consider an individual's needs and if they are being met to receive what you are trying to communicate. Can you imagine trying to build a house without certain materials like shingles, cement, or wood? Within one season, the house would not serve its purpose because the requirements were not met for the house to be adequately built.

For peace and purpose to be attained, you need connection and a relationship with yourself and others. This is how chaos becomes divine perfection: it allows our decisions to impact our lives beyond what we can see, with ripples of lessons reorienting us toward peace and purpose. Each connection is an opportunity that we can leverage to attain peace and purpose, as long as we understand how love plays a crucial role in everything. Communicating and understanding needs help to reduce distractions and noise when we interact with people. The journey of peace and purpose can yield abundance more readily when we see opportunities beyond ourselves.

Reflection

To ensure you understand the book of love and recognize what is at stake if you do not pursue inner peace and the purpose of your life, reflect on the following:

1. Have I consistently used my definition of love to hold myself and others accountable?

2. What must I start, stop, and keep doing to ensure that my communication is clear?

3. What is my indication that the needs of others or myself are not being met, preventing progress from being made?

Application

After reflecting on your answers to the above questions, journal about these responses for at least fifteen minutes per day. If you need more time to reflect and journal, do so; this is your opportunity to check your understanding of love and what's at stake when a journey of peace and purpose is not taken.

Book of Meditation

The most sacred place I have found during this human experience is within the stillness of my inner self. This place of peace allows us to go places where our human expression cannot take us, especially considering that our purpose is spiritual. Knowing how to leverage the strength of our limitless spiritual expression is important, because life cannot be solely navigated through our physical lens. Consistent behaviors that lean toward living life through our spiritual lens make a life of peace and purpose more easily attainable. Giving future generations the awareness and lessons learned from this human experience is life changing, allowing them to quickly get to a life of abundance.

- *Chapter of Grounding*

    ○ Quote—"Time is an illusion that has conditioned us to be productive. How can we be productive when our thoughts are in the past or future, and our bodies are present?" (*Love and Meditation: The Keys to Manifestation*, p.61)

    ○ Mantra—I am at peace at all times, and it feels still.

- *Chapter of Meditation*

    ○ Quote—"If I could stop the world from moving, I am sure people wouldn't notice. The movement of the world doesn't make people move; people make themselves move." (*Love and Meditation: The Keys to Manifestation*, p.69)

- ○ Mantra—I am meditating in a place beyond space and time where things are clear.

- *Chapter of Visualization*

  - ○ Quote—"What can be seen with my eye is not what I desire because it is already here. What I desire is a step beyond what my mind can fathom; it feels good to know that what is possible is within reach, as I already see it with my spiritual eyes." (*Love and Meditation: The Keys to Manifestation*, p.76)

  - ○ Mantra—I clearly see the life of peace and purpose I desire to live.

- *Chapter of Posture*

  - ○ Quote—"Sitting incorrectly can limit oxygen intake; our posture must be correct to maximize what we are capable of." (*Love and Meditation: The Keys to Manifestation*, p.79)

  - ○ Mantra—I give myself permission to experience emotions, mindful of my reaction.

- *Chapter of Manifestation*

  - ○ Quote—"If I think to breathe at my own pace before I change my pace of breath, which ultimately changes my breathing, I can obtain what I genuinely desire before working toward it." (*Love and Meditation: The Keys to Manifestation*, p.89)

  - ○ Mantra—I live an abundant life of peace and purpose, and it feels fulfilling.

Hindsight

Knowing that peace and purpose are at stake, I understand why meditation is needed during this human experience. Meditation, just like love, is what you define it as. For me, it allows access to a place that is unconnected from space and time, yet within my control. It is an inner peace that is not tangibly connected to this human experience. Meditation is the gateway to our spiritual expression, or highest sense of self, taking the lead and navigating this human experience more effectively.

I love grounding exercises, because they allow me to force myself to be present regardless of where I am or whom I am with. Our senses are always present, as they are designed to keep us alive during this human experience. They are not stimulated by what has happened or will happen; they are stimulated by what is happening now. What you may be triggered by or start thinking about is connected to what we have defined as the past and future, stimulating our senses to protect our body in the present as if what has happened or could happen is happening now. I love sitting on the porch, feeling and listening to the wind, watching clouds slowly scurry by, and feeling the sun's warmth.

These types of things happening in the present moment disrupt thoughts or thinking so that we can open the door of our inner spiritual expression through meditation. I love visiting this place within myself, as it allows me the safety to do necessary work during the journey of peace and purpose. Without judgment or fear, I reflect or ask questions to unpack and resolve so that I can move forward with the lesson learned. Our spiritual expression, connected to an unlimited source, gives us access to everything we need. We are often not in the space to receive it due to trying to survive. This is why we must understand the bigger picture, go on a journey of self, be love in action, and meditate consistently.

Peace is like watching the storm clouds go by without questioning the how and when or trying to control it. Purpose is the storm clouds being of service to the earth even when it may cause damage, interrupt plans, or not fit into what is perceived as possible. The balance of the two creates an ongoing harmonic cycle that allows an individual piece of life to serve a more significant cause, even through hurt and pain. I can only grasp this abstract concept because of meditation, allowing my highest sense to lead and piece things together in a way that I understand within my human expression's ability to comprehend. I also love meditation because it allows us the freedom to visualize in great detail beyond what we can do with our hands or see what's in front of us.

Manifesting a life of peace and purpose can be done only with good intent and through consistent decisions that align with what you visualize in specifics and define as peace and purpose. We must loosen our grip on how and when it will happen, as we could not possibly control or comprehend what happens beyond our lives. This is why chaos is truly divine perfection, allowing the ripples of our decisions to bring the necessary circumstances and people to help us attain what we desire even when it doesn't seem that way on the surface. Understanding this rhythm of life is like finding a rare diamond that you hold on to, perfecting the process of how you found the diamond to repeat, yet still maintain the diamond for a greater purpose. As you perfect that process, it is your posture or how you position yourself mentally to remain optimistic and open to the possibility that creates less resistance to the outcome.

Manifestation is not simply wishing for something and waiting for it to come. Manifesting is diving headfirst into each opportunity that time and chance provide. It is constantly making decisions from a place of peace in alignment with what you visualize; hopefully peace and purpose. It is applying lessons learned while leveraging gifts and talents. All of this is done while unconcerned about how and when things will happen, resting in the protection of your positive intention. Do your part on the journey of peace and purpose, and allow chaos to do the rest; abundance will follow.

Reflection

To ensure you understand the book of meditation and recognize what is at stake if you do not pursue inner peace and the purpose of your life, reflect on the following:

1. How can I integrate grounding exercises in my life to remain present as often as possible?

2. How can I integrate meditation in my life to create a consistent habit of going inward to get the necessary answers to move forward?

3. What can I do to exercise my creative muscle?

4. What can I start, stop, and keep doing to ensure I maintain the right posture throughout life?

5. What must I do to create a habit of making consistent and conscious choices, rooted in positive intent, that align with what I am trying to manifest, hopefully peace and purpose?

Application

After reflecting on your answers to the above questions, journal about these responses for at least fifteen minutes per day. If you need more time to reflect and journal, do so; this is your opportunity to check your understanding of meditation and what's at stake when a journey of peace and purpose is not taken.

Dear Future Generation,

I hope you can see and appreciate the work that has been done to ensure you have a life of abundance. It is now your turn to take what has been given to you to allow you to quickly find inner peace and your purpose in life to do the same for future generations. Before you reach adulthood or before you are even born, life will not be the same for you as it is for me. Know that the efforts to provide you with this compass to navigate life are rooted in unconditional love.

Find inner peace so you can operate from a place of clarity and love. Identify and honor your purpose in life so that you can be of service to people, making their lives a little easier. Trust the process, knowing that everything you need is being pulled from within as you encounter circumstances and people. Be comfortable with releasing to receive so that you carry what is relevant to your inner peace and purpose. Chase purpose so that everything can follow, leading you to a life of abundance and fulfillment.

Conclusion

Life does not stop with us. It is a continuous spectrum of ongoing events that those who follow us will experience. Do you care to help positively shape the experience of those who come behind you? What would it mean to help those behind you live a life of abundance when you may not have had the same chance? Those of us who live now have learned, based on our individual life experiences, that this human experience is challenging.

With that being said, give yourself permission to be human, knowing that you will make mistakes. Consider the ripple you will create that eventually comes back to you with every decision you make. Even when you ask for things, knowingly and unknowingly, see the lesson in every circumstance and person you encounter. Navigate life more efficiently by creating a harmonic rhythm between your human and spiritual expressions. Even though you can do whatever you want with your life, know that a journey of peace and purpose will sustain the outcome of your life for those who follow.

I challenge you to live a life of peace and purpose, helping to positively yet indirectly shape the life experiences that others will have. Even though this journey will not be easy, the harvest you reap will sustain you beyond what you think possible. The harvest of a thousand generations that follow is at stake when we do not live a life of peace and purpose. Life experiences you have gone through may repeat during the lives of those who follow you, becoming generational, limiting the potential of their own lives unless they break free through SCRAG. Although I am nothing close to perfection, I choose to show up with my best self, making consistent and conscious choices in alignment with inner peace and life's purpose for my future generations.